Baby's Babble!
Baby's First Sight Words

Baby & Toddler First Word Books

BABY PROFESSOR

EDUCATION KIDS

Speedy Publishing LLC

40 E. Main St. #1156

Newark, DE 19711

www.speedypublishing.com

Copyright 2016

Sight Words

all

Search and encircle the word.

all	so	you	all
a	all	also	will
all	up	all	with

Rewrite the word.

and

Search and encircle the word.

and	us	come	work
and	we	and	and
be	and	from	your

Rewrite the word.

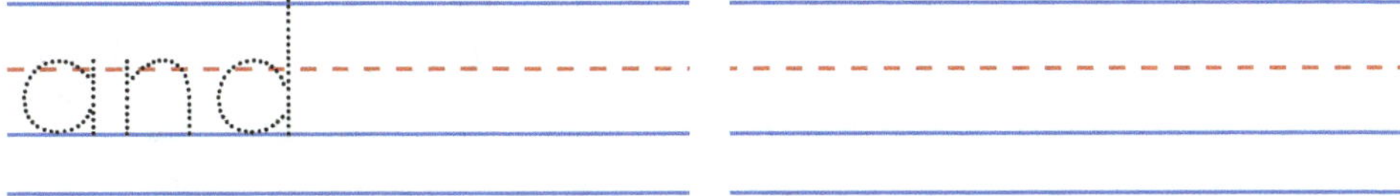

and

any

Search and encircle the word.

by	any	give	any
do	any	any	after
go	but	have	could

Rewrite the word.

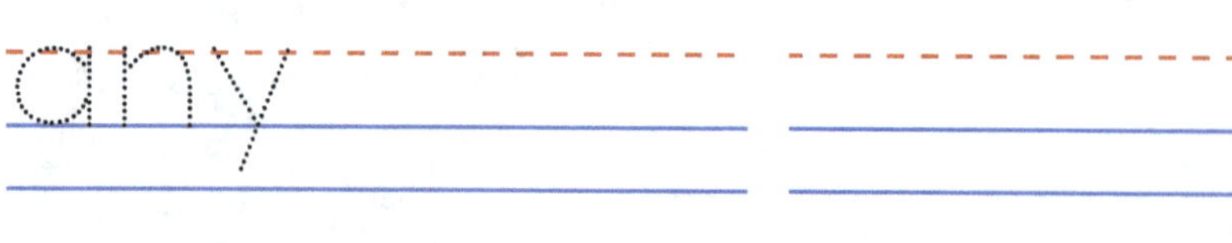

but

Search and encircle the word.

he	but	but	first
but	day	just	but
in	for	but	their

Rewrite the word.

but

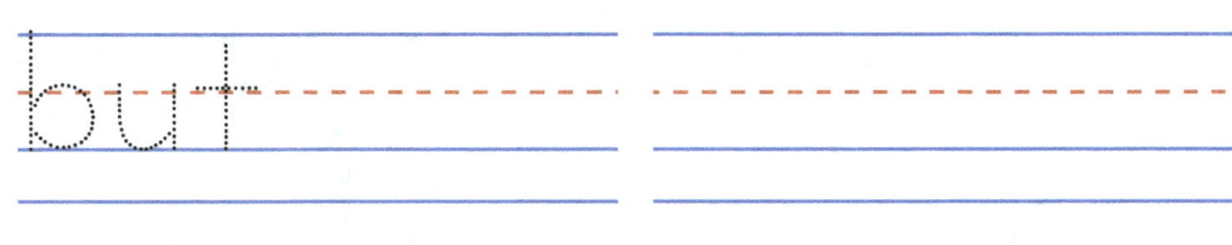

can

Search and encircle the word.

it	can	like	there
can	can	can	can
my	him	make	want

Rewrite the word.

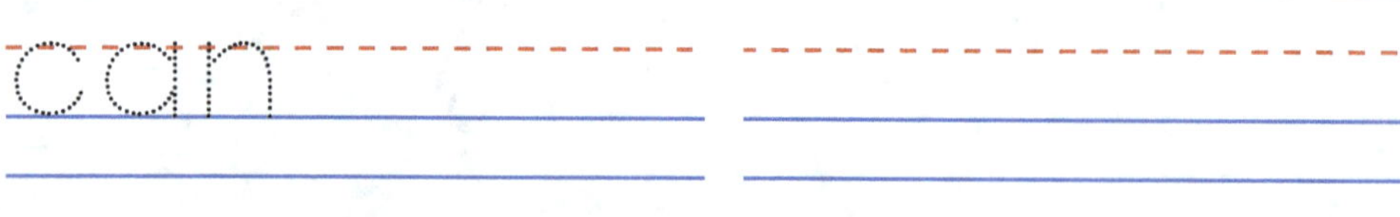

can

day

Search and encircle the word.

day	his	most	day
day	day	only	what
on	its	over	day

Rewrite the word.

day

for

Search and encircle the word.

not	for	her	look
now	for	for	for
one	for	his	most

Rewrite the word.

get

Search and encircle the word.

our	get	how	get
out	get	get	over
get	or	new	some

Rewrite the word.

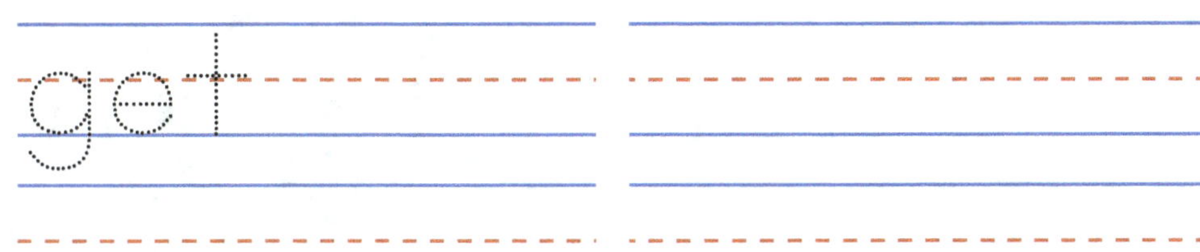

get

her

Search and encircle the word.

see	her	but	have
her	he	her	her
the	her	day	just

Rewrite the word.

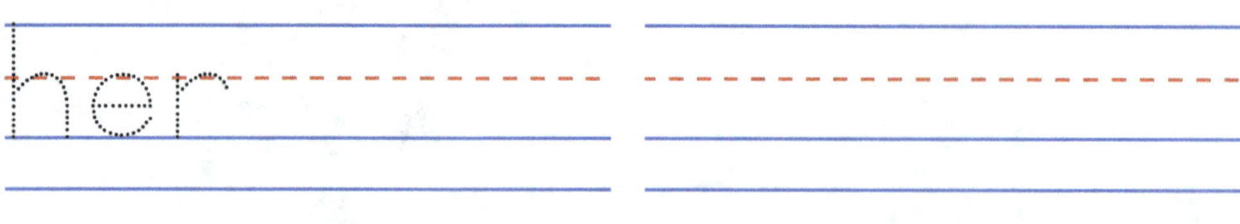

him

Search and encircle the word.

him	in	him	know
use	him	get	him
way	him	so	you

Rewrite the word.

his

Search and encircle the word.

who	a	to	his
take	his	up	his
his	as	his	come

Rewrite the word.

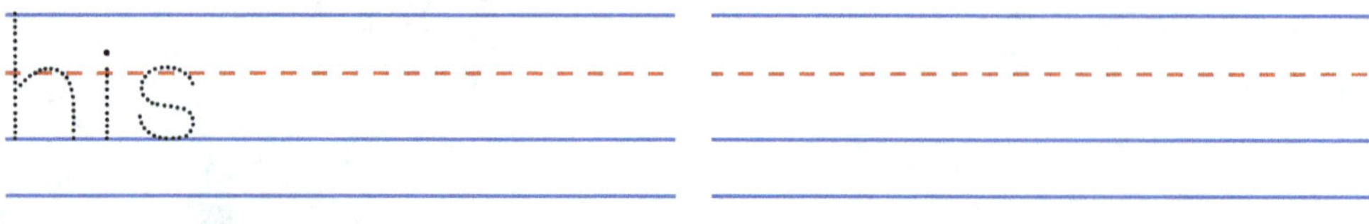

his

how

Search and encircle the word.

how	at	we	how
how	how	all	from
then	how	and	give

Rewrite the word.

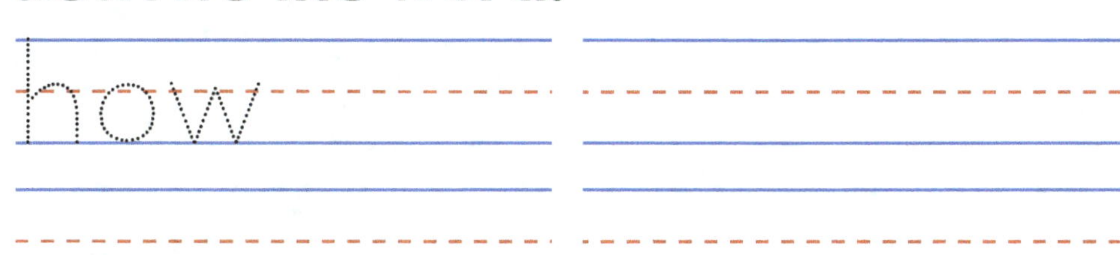

its

Search and encircle the word.

if	day	just	its
in	its	its	its
it	its	like	there

Rewrite the word.

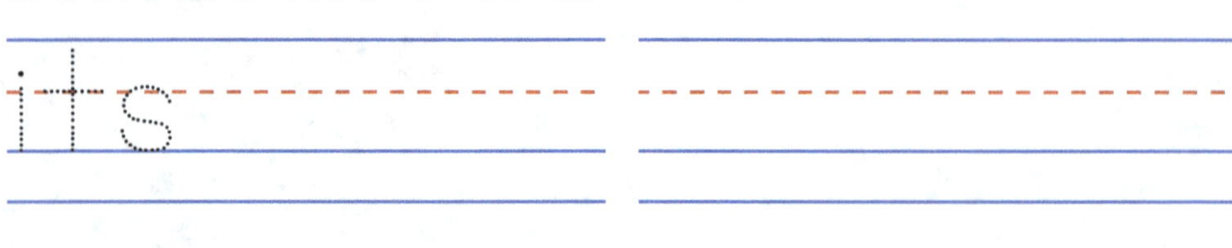

its

new

Search and encircle the word.

new	so	you	new
new	new	also	will
an	up	new	with

Rewrite the word.

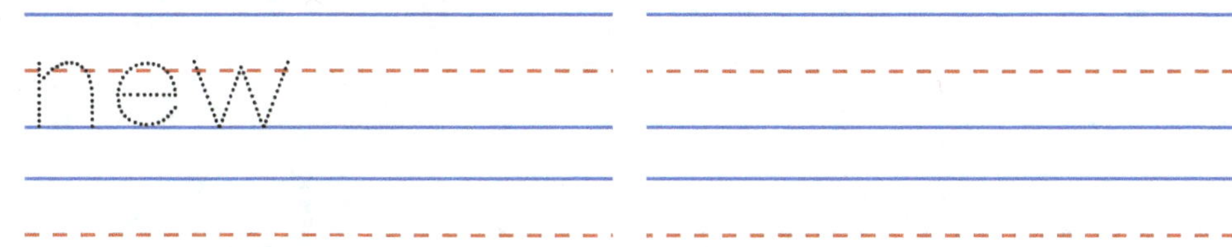

not

Search and encircle the word.

not	us	come	not
not	her	not	these
not	him	make	want

Rewrite the word.

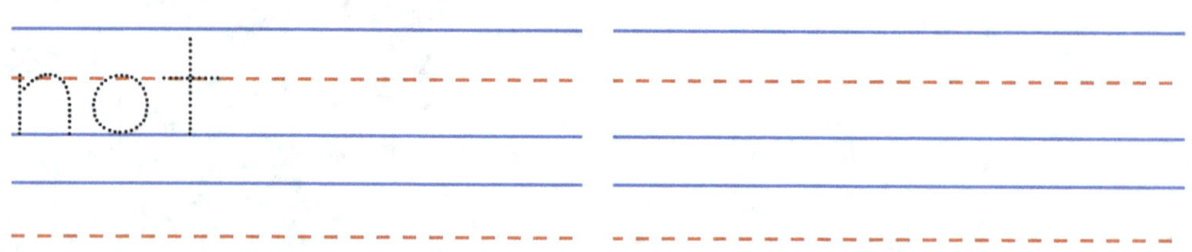

now

Search and encircle the word.

go	but	have	could
now	can	now	first
now	day	now	now

Rewrite the word.

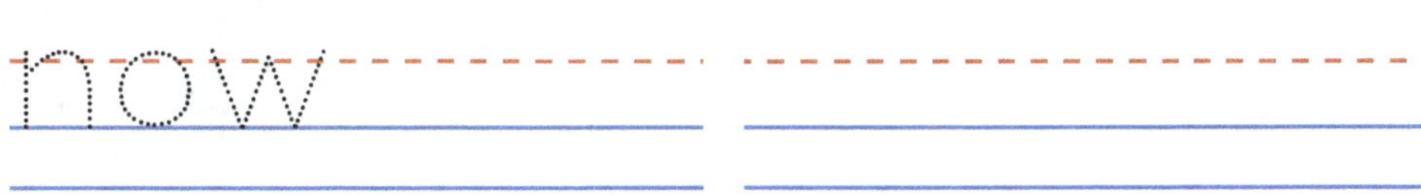

now

one

Search and encircle the word.

in	one	know	their
one	get	like	there
one	one	into	first

Rewrite the word.

our

Search and encircle the word.

if	our	just	other
our	for	our	our
it	our	like	there

Rewrite the word.

our

out

Search and encircle the word.

out	out	other	use
for	know	their	way
out	out	there	out

Rewrite the word.

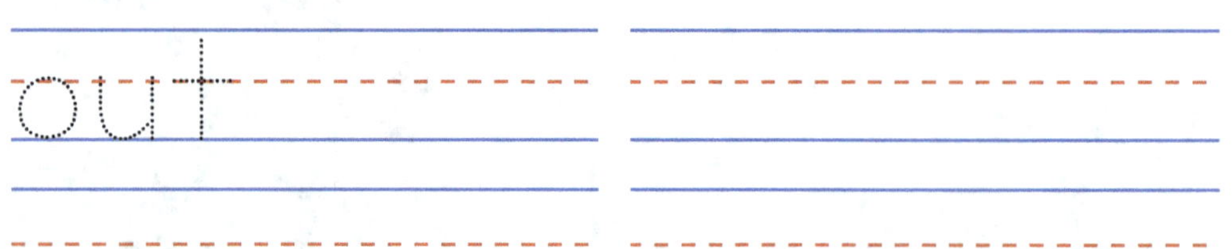

say

Search and encircle the word.

say	say	on	say
your	say	or	new
about	say	say	but

Rewrite the word.

see

Search and encircle the word.

first	see	in	see
see	use	it	get
see	way	see	so

Rewrite the word.

she

Search and encircle the word.

she	she	a	to
these	take	she	she
want	she	as	us

Rewrite the word.

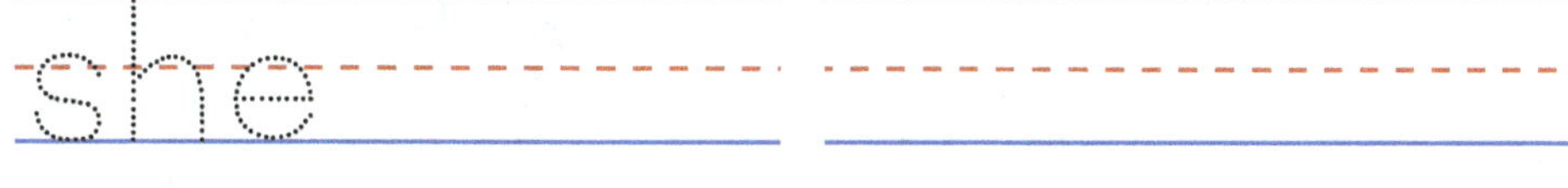

the

Search and encircle the word.

the	them	be	all
this	the	by	the
the	they	the	any

Rewrite the word.

two

Search and encircle the word.

go	two	have	could
two	can	two	two
if	two	just	other

Rewrite the word.

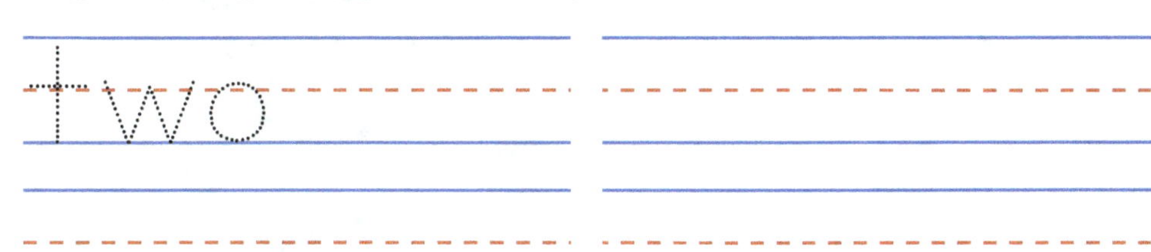

two

use

Search and encircle the word.

use	know	use	way
get	like	use	use
use	you	when	not

Rewrite the word.

way

Search and encircle the word.

way	also	way	way
way	back	with	one
us	come	work	way

Rewrite the word.

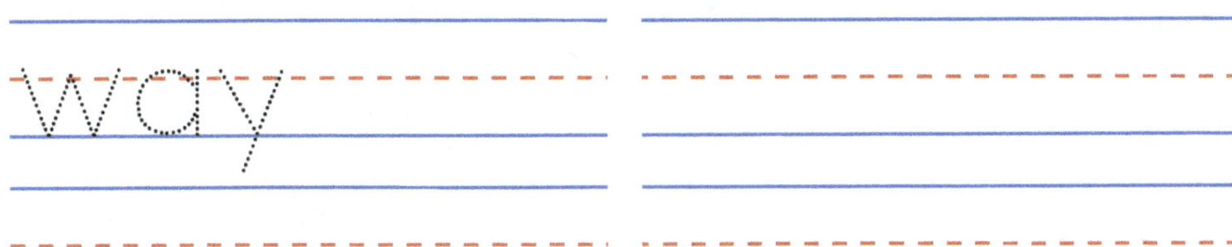

who

Search and encircle the word.

who	even	who	who
all	who	your	say
and	give	who	see

Rewrite the word.

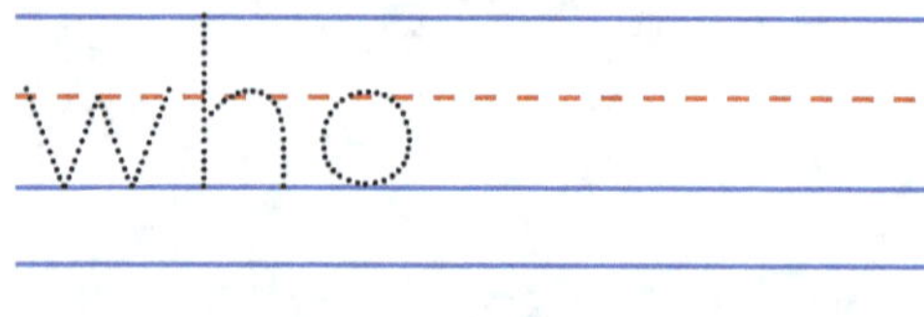

YOU

Search and encircle the word.

you	you	first	two
day	just	you	you
you	know	their	way

Rewrite the word.

also

Search and encircle the word.

also	that	at	we
what	them	also	all
also	also	by	also

Rewrite the word.

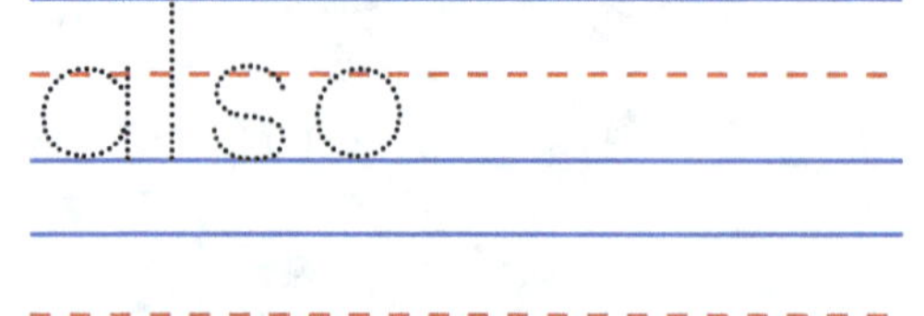

back

Search and encircle the word.

us	back	work	our
we	even	back	back
back	from	your	back

Rewrite the word.

come

Search and encircle the word.

come	what	come	be
over	come	come	by
some	come	they	do

Rewrite the word.

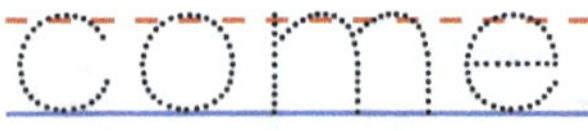

even

Search and encircle the word.

by	and	give	even
even	even	good	after
even	but	have	even

Rewrite the word.

even

from

Search and encircle the word.

from	so	you	when
from	from	also	from
an	up	back	from

Rewrite the word.

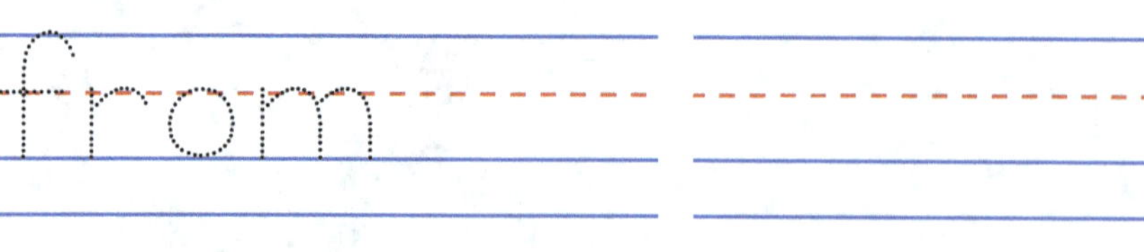

give

Search and encircle the word.

two	day	give	other
use	give	give	their
way	give	like	give

Rewrite the word.

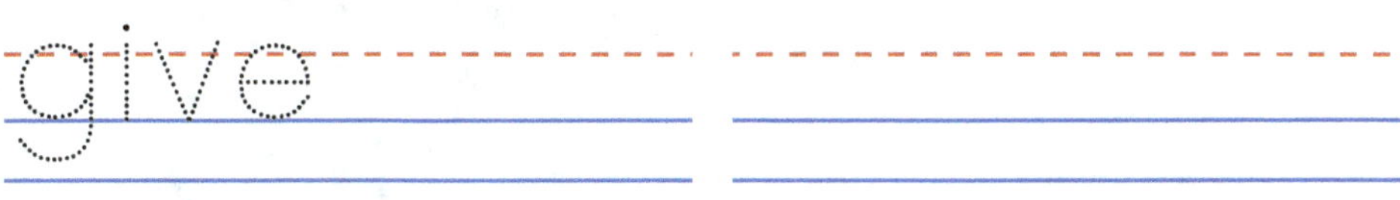

good

Search and encircle the word.

two	good	good	want
use	his	most	well
good	good	only	good

Rewrite the word.

have

Search and encircle the word.

have	and	have	about
take	any	good	have
than	have	have	have

Rewrite the word.

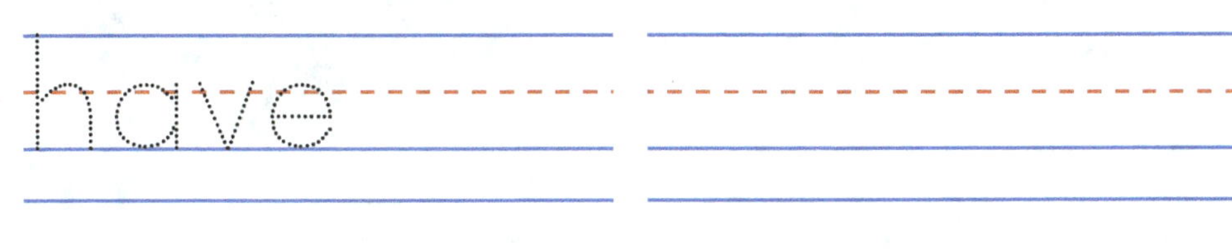

Visit
BABY PROFESSOR
EDUCATION KIDS
www.BabyProfessorBooks.com
to download Free Baby Professor eBooks
and view our catalog of new and exciting
Children's Books